Thirty Points of Love

Thirty Points of Love

Better Thoughts. Better Relationships.
A Better You.

by

Eric von Mizener

Hamilton & Hunter
2013

Cover Designer – Arial Burnz

Published by
Hamilton & Hunter
PO Box 7342
Moreno Valley, CA 92552

For everyone who stuck by me
when worldly wisdom would suggest otherwise.
Your patience is a lesson in love.

Introduction: Read This First

Nearly a decade after the collapse of my second marriage, I'd been through a series of relationships and wild times. And too many breakups. Being accused of spreading herpes was upsetting, but disproven by lab results. A girlfriend assaulting me with a bayonet was truly frightening. And coming home to find I lived alone brought me to my knees.

This time, however, was ninety-five percent perfect. It was the five percent hell that did us in for the third time in two years. And it was the same pattern playing out – the disagreements, the fights and the lonely disintegration. What was supposed to be building us up was sucking us dry. I knew things had to change. But I didn't know how.

I eschewed the sofa and sat on the floor next to the coffee table. I took a sip of cocoa – it needed bit more brandy – picked up a pen and I wrote that *I will not raise my voice. I do not need to raise my voice to be heard.*

Beneath that I wrote *I do not need to "win."* And I kept writing. I didn't know where this was coming from, but I went with it. I wrote the things I hadn't seen. The things I hadn't listened to. All the things that I'd been doing wrong. Well, not *all* the things – God is still showing me those. But enough to exhaust my spirit and my emotions. I wasn't used to being that honest with myself. Later while going through them, I found they broke down into thirty points. One for each day of the month.

But for all I worked on myself, I knew it wouldn't change my former girlfriend. The change in me might affect the way she perceived me or responded to me, but only to a point. And she was a reasonable woman.

If you are in a relationship, don't expect anything in this book to change the person you are involved with. Only they can do that. And if you are involved with a sociopath, a narcissist, an addict, etc. pray for them, but do not expect change. No one is beyond God's redemption, but first they have to want it. And to want it, they have to realize they need it. What lights the pilot light of change is different from person to person.

Also, regarding pronouns, these points are all written from a male point of view. That was done for two simple reasons. I am male and they were written for my own introspection, much like a diary entry.

Reading these on a daily basis has helped me tremendously. When I've gone awhile without referring to them each morning, I see that difference too. These aren't rules or laws, but they point me in the right direction. I also suggest making plenty of notes. See where you are, what you need to work on. When you come back each month, you can see your progress and be encouraged. It is a process.

And, yes, there are more points to love than these. But these are what helped me, and I'm sure they can help you too.

Eric von Mizener
Great Lent, 2013

Day 1

I will not raise my voice. I do not need to raise my voice to be heard.

Day 2

I do not need to "win." It is better to be a good man and to do my best. All else is in God's hands and outside my control.

Day 3

I might disagree, but I will disagree with respect.

Day 4

When I disagree I will simultaneously reaffirm – to myself and to her – that I still love her, I still want her, I still know that she's "the one."

Day 5

I will accept her frustrations without becoming defensive or angry.

Day 6

I will let her know when a boundary has been crossed – not ruminate on it, becoming ornery or building up to an explosion.

I will respect her when she tells me a boundary has been crossed, without becoming defensive or plowing ahead, either to vent or to "win." Rather, I will feel sorrow for having hurt the one I love.

Day 8

When I feel hurt by something she has done, but find myself dumbfounded (which is common for me), I will walk away from anger or snideness.

Instead, I will collect my thoughts so that I may calmly express myself in due time and proper place.

Day 9

I will reaffirm my love, my commitment and my desire.

Day 10

I will not say "it's time to call it a relationship." Rather, I will say "I love you, I want you and I believe that you're the one; I think that you are wonderful, but we need to find another way to relate to each other because what we are doing is not working."

Day 11

I will support all of her desires or endeavours that don't cause harm or ask me to violate my ethics or morals.

Day 12

Past loves, hers and mine, will be only in the past, like a lost civilization interesting only as history, but dead to the present.

Day 13

Forgiven hurts will remain forgiven. They will not be spoken of again.

If a pattern emerges of hurtful behavior, I will mention that this seems to be/is becoming a pattern. I will not mention previous incidents (she knows them) unless she asks.

If she asks, I will mention how the current and forgiven instance(s) demonstrate a pattern, but stick to the present issue and how to avoid the pattern from intruding into the future.

I will not say "this is like when you did X, Y or Z."

And, if she suggests a pattern in my behavior, I will not become defensive. I will assume the past is still forgiven; her concern is the present incident and how to avoid its reoccurrence in the future.

Day 15

All reasonable boundaries and desires may be discussed and renegotiated whenever either person feels that their needs or wants have changed or are in flux.

Day 16

The relationship – and I with it – shall remain fluid, able to adapt to the persons in it and to the situations encountered, together or as individuals.

Hurts from old models of relating to each other will not be brought up.

Day 17

God is more important than she is. At no other time will I ever say anything is more important than she is.

Day 18

I will respect her different understanding of God, and her separate relationship with Him. I am but a child in Christ, and our love for Him is more important than our understanding of He who surpasses all understanding.[1]

[1] Philippians 4:7.

Day 19

When I feel insecure, vulnerable or slighted, I will expose my vulnerability to her, rather than engage in defensive, self–protective behavior. I will lay down my arms, my loud words and winning arguments. I will try instead, like an innocent child, to express my hurt and allow her to apologize and/or explain the situation.

Day 20

I will not hold onto old hurts. Scars are not signs of wounds, but of the beautiful healing God has given us.

Day 21

I will reaffirm my love, desire and commitment. I will do this daily. Even if times are bad; even if my heart grows feint. Times improve and hearts grow stronger (or can even be replaced[2] – as I know so well).

[2] Psalm 51:10.

Day 22

I will not let waves of my enthusiasm drown out her voice or what she has to say.

Other men may pursue her; family, friends and others (well–intentioned or not) might try to turn her from me.

I will be stronger and better than those who would turn her. I will remain romantic and thoughtful. I will not be jealous, but honestly voice insecurity if it occurs.

If I treat her as well as when she chose me, she will not be turned. (And if she does turn, it will be her choice and weakness – not mine.)

Likewise, I will not allow others to turn me away from her.

Day 24

I will not be proud. I will be willing to apologize for any hurt. Her tears are as much a part of her – just as golden and just as important – as her laughter.

I will pray for her daily. And for me to be a calm man, slow to anger and quick to forgive.

Day 26

I will step back from my own feelings, put myself in her shoes, and try to act with the same love and respect that I would want (even if she prefers it expressed differently than I do). There will be time to discuss my feelings later.

I will not forget to discuss my feelings. Ignoring my own feelings is just as harmful as ignoring hers. (See Day 6.)

None of this restricts me from being the man that God has made me – or from using and enjoying His gifts.

Day 29

None of this restricts her from being the woman that God has made her – or from using and enjoying His gifts.

Each day I will tell her "I love you."

Day 31

When the month has thirty-one days – or twenty-eight or twenty-nine, such as February – I use the last day of the month to review all thirty points. This helps to maintain balance. It allows me to do a quick overall check of myself and my relationship. Although a former hot head, it is now a rare day on which I raise my voice. But I still have other weaknesses on the list. It's a process.

The review also helps remind me why I wrote them and the purpose they serve. Because it is not my purpose to no longer raise my voice, to learn about boundaries or to engage in discussions properly. All these things are good, but they are good because they serve my real purpose – and that is to have a loving and harmonious relationship that glorifies my God.

NOTES

NOTES

NOTES

NOTES

www.ingramcontent.com/pod-product-compliance
Lightning Source LLC
Chambersburg PA
CBHW020516030426
42337CB00011B/422